EMBRACING SPIRITUAL AWAKENING

Diana Butler Bass
on the Dynamics of Experiential Faith

A 5-Session Study by Diana Butler Bass with Tim Scorer

Scripture quotations are from the New Revised Standard Version Bible. © 1989 by the Division of Christian Education of the National Council of Churches of Christ in the USA. Used by permission.

Morehouse Education Resources,
a division of Church Publishing Incorporated
Editorial Offices: 600 Grant Street, Suite 630, Denver, CO 80203

For catalogs and orders call:
1-800-672-1789
www.MorehouseEducation.org

Photos on pages 11, 12, 27, 28, 45, 46, 59, 60, 75 and 76 © 2013 by Dirk deVries. All rights reserved. Cover photo by Rob Cannon Photography, Alexandria, VA. Used with permission.

ISBN-13: 978-1-60674-114-6

"*Embracing Spiritual Awakening* invites participants to examine and understand the changing cultural landscape in North America. Is the oft-heard critique of declining numbers in congregations simply a canard of those who would prefer a world of families with many children and stay-at-home mothers, or is it the consequence of increasing ethnic and cultural and religious diversity around us? Or is it something else? Diana Butler Bass leads a discussion of what it means to be spiritual, to be religious, and how Christians today might be grace-filled witnesses to the reality they know and experience."

—The Most Rev. Katharine Jefferts Schori
Presiding Bishop & Primate of The Episcopal Church

"Led by one of today's foremost interpreters of Christianity, *Embracing Spiritual Awakening* provides a rich and engaging educational and spiritual experience."

—Marcus Borg
popular author, and Canon Theologian,
Trinity Episcopal Church, Portland, OR

"Diana Butler Bass is a great "awakener" among us. She refers to two "awakenings," a spiritual newness that comes from beyond us, and a sociological recognition of our new social circumstance. More than that, Bass brings her vocation of awakening to concrete practice in ways that make a difference to real people. No more slumbering!"

—Walter Brueggemann
Columbia Theological Seminary

"Filled with both hope and very specific and practical observations, *Embracing Spiritual Awakening* is a tour d' force by a superb scholar at the top of her game."

—Phyllis Tickle
author, lecturer, and workshop leader

"Diana Butler Bass is one of the finest thinkers and educators I've ever met. She combines the insight of a scholar of religious history with the foresight of a keen social analyst. Groups and individuals who care about the future of their churches will find in *Embracing Spiritual Awakening* a choice and high-quality resource—not only for individual and group study, but also for creating communities of practice who become the change that is needed in our churches."

—Brian D. McLaren
author/speaker

TABLE OF CONTENTS

QUICK GUIDE TO THIS HANDBOOK

TEN things to know as you begin to work with this resource:

1. HANDBOOK + WORKBOOK

This handbook is a guide to the group process as well as a workbook for everyone in the group.

2. A FIVE-SESSION RESOURCE

Each of the five sessions presents a distinct topic for focused group study and conversation.

3. DVD-BASED RESOURCE

The teaching content in each session comes in the form of input by Diana Butler Bass and response by members of a small group on a DVD recording of just over 30 minutes in length.

4. EVERYONE GETS EVERYTHING

This handbook addresses everyone in the group, not one group leader. There is no separate "Leader's Guide."

5. GROUP FACILITATION

The creators of this resource assume that someone will be designated as group facilitator for each session. You may choose the same person or a different person for each of the five sessions.

6. TIME FLEXIBILITY

Each of the five sessions is flexible and can be between one hour and two or more hours in length: however, if you intend to cover all the material presented, you will need the full two hours.

7. BUILD YOUR OWN SESSION

Prior to the session it is advisable for one or more members of the group to determine what to include in the group meeting time. In some cases the session outline presents options from which you can choose. In other cases the material is organized as a progression through the three or four main topics presented by Diana Butler Bass.

8. WITHIN EACH TOPIC IN A SESSION

Each segment in a session features a mix of input from Diana Butler Bass and the other members of the small group in the video, plus questions for discussion or other creative activities to guide individual and group reflection.

9. BEFORE THE SESSION

Each session opens with five activities for participants to use as personal preparation prior to the session.

10. CLOSING AND BEYOND

Each session ends with an option that is a suggestion for ongoing personal engagement with the topic of the session. A closing prayer is provided. Groups are encouraged to follow a prayer practice that reflects their own traditions and experience.

BEYOND THE "QUICK GUIDE"

Helpful information and guidance for anyone using this resource:

1. HANDBOOK + WORKBOOK

This handbook is a guide to the group process as well as a workbook for everyone in the group.

- We hope the handbook gives you all the information you need to feel confident in shaping the program to work for you and your fellow group members.
- The workspace provided in the handbook encourages you...
  — to respond to leading questions.
  — to write or draw your own reflections.
  — to note the helpful responses of other group members.

2. FIVE-SESSION RESOURCE

This resource presents Diana Butler Bass's insights on Spiritual Awakening, framed as five distinct topics of study:

1. Waking Up
2. Believing
3. Behaving
4. Belonging
5. Awakening

3. DVD-BASED RESOURCE

The teaching content in each session comes in the form of input by Diana Butler Bass and response by members of a small group; just over 30 minutes in length.

Diana Butler Bass's focused presentations and accessible academic authority stimulates thoughtful and heartfelt conversation among her listeners.

The edited conversations present group sharing that builds on Diana's initial teaching. They are intended to present to you a model of small group interaction that is personal, respectful and engaged.

- You will notice that the participants in the DVD group also become our teachers. In many cases, quotes from the group members enrich the teaching component of this resource. This will also happen in your group—you will become teachers for one another.
- We hope that the DVD presentations spark conversations about those things that matter most to those who are advancing the enterprise of interfaith cooperation in the 21st Century.

4. EVERYONE GETS EVERYTHING

The handbook addresses everyone in the group, not one group leader. There is no separate "Leader's Guide."

Unlike many small-group resources, this one makes no distinction between material for the group facilitator and for the participants. Everyone has it all! We believe this empowers you and your fellow group members to share creatively in the leadership.

5. GROUP FACILITATION

We designed this for you to designate a group facilitator for each session. It does not have to be the same person for all five sessions, because everyone has all the material. It is, however, essential that you and the other group members are clear about who is facilitating each session. One or two people still have to be responsible for these kinds of things:

- making arrangements for the meeting space (see notes on Meeting Space, p. 13)
- setting up the space to be conducive to conversations in a diverse, small-group community
- creating and leading an opening to the session (see notes on Opening, p. 13)
- helping the group decide on which elements of the guide to focus on in that session
- facilitating the group conversation for that session
- keeping track of the time
- calling the group members to attend to the standards established for the group life (see notes on Group Standards, p. 13)
- creating space in the conversation for all to participate
- keeping the conversation moving along so that the group covers all that it set out to do
- ensuring that time is taken for a satisfying closing to the session
- making sure that everyone is clear about date, location and focus for the next session
- following up with people who missed the session

6. TIME FLEXIBILITY

Each of the five sessions is flexible and can be between one hour and two or more hours in length: however, if you intend to cover all the material presented, you will need the full two hours.

We designed this resource for your group to tailor it to fit the space available in the life of the congregation or community using it. That might be Sunday morning for an hour before or after worship, two hours on a weekday evening, or 90 minutes on a weekday morning.

Some groups might decide to spend two sessions on one of the five major topics. There's enough material in each of the five outlines to do that. Rushing to get through more than the time comfortably allows, results in people not having the opportunity to speak about the things that matter to them.

7. BUILD YOUR OWN SESSION

Prior to the session, it is advisable for one or more members of the group to determine what to include in the group meeting time. In some cases the session outline presents options from which you can choose. In other cases the material is organized as a progression through the three or four main topics presented by Diana Butler Bass.

- One or two people might take on the responsibility of shaping the session based on what they think will appeal to the group members. This responsibility could be shared from week to week.
- The group might take time at the end of one session to look ahead and decide on what they will cover in the next session. In the interest of time, it might be best to assign this planning to a couple of members of the group.
- You might decide to do your personal preparation for the session (the five activities in 'Before the Session'), and when everyone comes together for the session, proceed on the basis of what topics interested people the most.

8. WITHIN EACH TOPIC IN A SESSION

Each segment in a session features a mix of input from Diana Butler Bass and the other members of the small group in the video, plus questions for discussion or other creative activities to guide individual and group reflection.

You will recognize that the activities and topics in the study guide emerge both from the structured teaching of Diana as well as the informal and spontaneous conversation of the group members. This parallels the process of your group, which will be initially led by the content of the DVD and the study guide, but then branch off in directions that emerge spontaneously from the particular life of your group.

9. BEFORE THE SESSION

Each session opens with five activities for participants to use as personal preparation prior to the session,

- We intend these activities to open in you some aspect of the topic being considered in the upcoming session. This may lead you to feel more confident when addressing the issue in the group.
- Sometimes these questions are the same as ones raised in the context of the session. They offer the opportunity for you to do some personal reflection both before and/or after engaging in the group conversation on that topic.

10. CLOSING AND BEYOND

Each session has a final reflective option for participants to take from the session and use as an extension of their learning. These offer a disciplined way for each participant to continue to harvest the riches of the group conversation.

A responsive closing prayer is provided at the end of each session. Groups are encouraged to follow a prayer practice that reflects their own traditions and experience.

Another aspect of closing is *evaluation*. This is not included in an intentional way in the design of the sessions; however, evaluation is such a natural and satisfying thing to do that it could be included as part of the discipline of closing each session. It's as simple as taking time to respond to these questions:

- What insights am I taking from this session?
- What contributed to my learning?
- What will I do differently as a result of my being here today?

POINTERS ON FACILITATION

1. MEETING SPACE

- Take time to prepare the space for the group. When people come into a space that has been prepared for them, they trust the hospitality, resulting in a willingness to bring the fullness of them into the conversation. Something as simple as playing recorded music as people arrive will contribute to this sense of "a space prepared for you."
- Think about how the space will encourage a spirit of reverence, intimacy and care. Will there be a table in the center of the circle where a candle can be lit each time the group meets? Is there room for other symbols that emerge from the group's life?

2. OPENING

- In the opening session, take time to go around the circle and introduce yourselves in some way.
- Every time a group comes together again, it takes each member time to feel fully included. Some take longer than others. An important function of facilitation is to help this happen with ease, so people find themselves participating fully in the conversation as soon as possible. We designed these sessions with this in mind. Encouraging people to share in the activity proposed under *Group Life* is one way of supporting that feeling of inclusion.
- The ritual of opening might include the lighting of a candle, an opening prayer, the singing of a hymn where appropriate, and the naming of each person present.

3. GROUP STANDARDS

- There are basic standards in the life of a group that are helpful to name when a new group begins. Once they are named, you can always come back to them as a point of reference if necessary. Here are two basics:
  - Everything that is said in this group remains in the group. *(confidentiality)*
  - We will begin and end at the time agreed. *(punctuality)*
- Are there any others that you need to name as you begin? Sometimes standards emerge from the life of the group and need to be named when they become evident, otherwise they are just assumed.

QUESTIONS OF AWAKENING

	CONVENTIONAL RELIGIOUS QUESTION	THE SPIRITUAL QUESTION
BELIEVING *(understanding)*	What do I (we) believe? *Creed and Dogma*	How do I (we) believe that? *Experience and Reason*
BEHAVING *(action)*	How do I (we) do that? *Rules and Techniques*	What should I (we) do now? *Discernment and Purpose*
Belonging *(identity)*	Who am I (are we)? *Membership and Choice*	Whose am I (are we)? *Relationship and Community*

*From the teaching of Diana Butler Bass

> **"** An awakening is a period of
> sustained religious and spiritual
> transformation that affects an
> entire culture. Whereas a *revival*
> alters the worldview of a single
> person, *awakening* alters the
> worldview of a culture. **"**

SESSION | 1

WAKING UP

BEFORE THE SESSION

Many participants like to come to the group conversation after considering individually some of the issues that will be raised. The following five reflective activities are intended to open your mind, memories and emotions regarding some aspects of this session's topic. Use the space provided here to note your reflections.

1. Why do people in America have a very different relationship with religion than people did 50 years ago? Why is it, for example, that way fewer people participate in Christian worship on a regular basis than did a few decades ago?

2. You know that the church is a very different place than it was in the 1950s and 1960s. What do you think and feel about that difference?

3. At least half the people in America know that they have had a mystical experience *(an experience of wonder or transcendence that enables them to know God—whatever they understand by that word—better and that gives them a clearer sense of who they are in the universe).* Remember times when you had what you would refer to as a mystical experience. Ask one or two other people about their personal experience of Mystery and Presence. As you listen to them, what insights about spirituality come to you?

4. In times of dramatic change and awakening, it matters how we view and talk about the past. You have at least two ways of viewing the past: "through rose-colored glasses" and "telling the truth about how it was." You probably do both. Which one do you tend to do more often? What difference does that make?

5. Take time to draw on a large sheet of paper your own journey of faith as a path with as many features as any path we might choose to walk (mountains, crossroads, bridges, valleys, rocky or smooth surfaces, forests and so on). Note key words or phrases to describe any of those places that have made up your pilgrimage of spirituality and religion. When you are done, share it with someone else and ask them to reflect back to you what they notice about your journey of faith and Spirit. *Feel free to use any art medium that appeals to you: collage, mixed media, charcoal, clay and so on.*

The theme of this volume of the *Embracing Series* is "Embracing Spiritual Awakening." You have come together as a group, ready to uncover some responses to this question: What are the dynamics of experiential faith in the second decade of the 21st century?

This is a new group, meeting for the first time. Take a few minutes to introduce yourselves in two ways:
- by telling your name
- by telling one thing that attracted you to participate in this program

In March of 2013, another group met in Alexandria, Virginia, to learn with Diana Butler Bass and to grapple with the same issues that are on your agenda for these five sessions.

Moving from left to right as you will see them on the screen, they are Marilyn Lightfoote, C.J. Reid, Sharon Watts, Diana Butler Bass, Alex Holm, Stephanie Campbell, Greg Millikin and Tim Scorer (moderator and author of this study guide). All except Tim are members of St. Paul's Episcopal Church in Alexandria. You won't hear from each person in every session, but over the course of five sessions you will hear contributions from all six participants in the St. Paul's group.

Play the first section of the DVD for Session 1, through Diana's presentation.

Note: Within this first presentation, Diana refers to two charts that you can find online:
- The Pew Research Center report on "Trends in Religious Affiliation, 2007–1012," http://www.pewforum.org/Unaffiliated/nones-on-the-rise.aspx
- The Public Religion Research Institute's chart on "The End of a White Christian Strategy," http://publicreligion.org/research/2012/11/american-values-post-election-survey-2012/

Diana uses the word *awakening* to describe something that is happening to people of faith all over the United States. She explains what she means by *awakening* in this religious context:

> *An* awakening *time is a period of sustained religious and spiritual transformation that affects an entire culture.*

Diana highlights aspects of the *awakening* in these six statements:
- The emerging generation is completely different in its composition with regard to its religious affiliation than any other generation ever in American history. Thirty-five percent of young adults under 30 claim to be unaffiliated with any religion.

- Forty percent of Americans under 40 are either part of a racially diverse group (for example, Hispanic, African-American, South Asian, Indian, Middle Eastern, African) or religiously diverse group (for example, Muslim, Hindu, Jewish, Buddhist). The traditional complex of what we understood religion to be in the U.S. (largely Christian, largely Protestant and Catholic, and historically majority white) is now 26% of the population.
- As Christianity moves out from this point in North America it will have to be conversant with "spiritual but not religious" as well as religious and racial pluralism. Those in the traditional Protestant-Catholic complex are going to have figure out how to remake faith in this context.
- There is no possible way demographically to return to church the way it looked in the 50s and 60s; it's historically impossible. Yet too many Christians want things to go back to the way they were. When we wake up we have to open our eyes and see the world around as it is.
- Almost half the population says that they are spiritual *and* religious. That means that somehow they want to retain some tie or connection with a conventional or traditional religious community, but they want it to be somehow different. They want it to meet their spiritual needs in a new and deeper way. (See chart titled *Are You Spiritual or Religious?* on p. 18.)

- This awakening is happening in a powerfully new context of pluralism and disaffiliation, but that doesn't mean that people are stopping their search for God. People are still strongly hungry to find God in their lives and to have lives of deep and profound meaning.

1. Using Diana's definition of *awakening* as *a period of sustained religious and spiritual transformation that affects an entire culture*, what have you observed that either supports Diana's observations noted above, or adds to them?

2. You have heard Diana expressing excitement and hope about what she sees happening in religion in America in these early years of the 21st century. What are you feeling about what is going on? How is this dramatic "awakening" affecting you and your faith community?

ARE YOU SPIRITUAL OR RELIGIOUS?

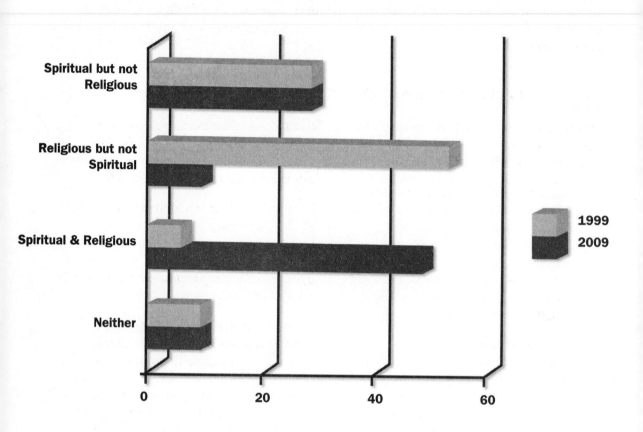

OPTIONS FOR FURTHER EXPLORATION

Before going on to choose from the following options for conversation and reflection, together watch the second part of the DVD for Session 1, in which Diana engages in conversation with the members of the group.

OPTION 1: WAKING UP TO RELIGION AND SPIRITUALITY

Sharon asks a key question about the difference between the words *religion* and *spirituality*. Diana offers this distinction:

> *When people in North America use the word* religion *they are specifically referring to an institution that has organized matters of faith and that cares about external things such as buildings, creeds, rule books and so on. People used to refer to this as "organized religion," but now it is just "religion."*
>
> *Spirituality is understood to be an experience of wonder and transcendence that makes people understand God (whatever they mean by that word) better and that gives them a clearer sense of who they are in the universe. Spirituality is a lot more subjective and internal—the more mystical part of faith.*

Diana then notes that today 49% of people in America claim to have had some kind of mystical experience in their lives. This is a much higher number than in 1960 when only 20% said they'd ever had a mystical experience. She notes that we live in a more experiential culture and that is showing up in the distinction between these two words, *religion* and *spirituality*.

Marilyn then wonders about the possibility that earlier on people felt less open to acknowledge that they had these experiences, and now they feel more comfortable talking about them. It may not be a difference in what happened, but a difference in the ability to express that.

Diana affirms that we now live in a more open environment where we feel free to share these things—to talk about what is going on inside in the deepest part of ourselves. People are freed up to share these experiential moments, even in more traditional churches.

1. This exploration of religion and spirituality provides a rich opportunity for people in a new small group to get to know one another. Use the time here to share with one another your own experiences of religion and spirituality. Because this is early in the life of this group when people may be anxious about speaking out in the large group, you might break up into pairs or triads for this conversation.

2. Choose one of these topics as a way to begin sharing:
   - I have come to appreciate the difference between religion and spirituality through…
   - An experience of mystery (wonder, God's presence, the sacred) that had great meaning for me was…
   - The way I make sense of the change in "spirituality and religion" from 1960 to the present time is…

Diana notes the three main reasons why people are leaving conventional religious organizations:
- Too much stress on money and power.
- Traditionally religious groups are overly focused on the rules to the detriment of Spirit.
- Religion has become overly politicized. (This critique is especially made with regard to the religious right in the U.S.)

1. Which of these has been influential in changes in your congregation's membership?

Diana then adds:

> *We know what they don't like, so the question now is, "Where are they going?" How are people re-organizing their lives? We just don't have a clear picture of that yet.*

3. Where do you think people are going when they leave religious organizations, knowing that they want to get away from the stress on money, power, rules and politics, and become more aligned with Spirit?

2. Which of these three issues has been influential in your relationship with religious organizations?

OPTION 3: WAKING UP TAKES PRACTICE

Stephanie compares the awakening experience to what it takes to wake up in the morning, "When I wake up I'm groggy and need coffee." She wonders if the younger generation—like her three young adult children—may have the ability to open their eyes and get going in a new time without coffee. They don't experience the grogginess of her generation. Then she notes, "Diana, I was impressed with your hopefulness and the way you are looking at the future with such great expectation."

Her wondering leads Diana to this reflection on spiritual grounding through practice:

> *When we're afraid we don't want to look at the reality around us. When we look back we want to look through rose-colored glasses.*
>
> *An important spiritual practice in waking up is to develop a clearer vision both ahead and around, seeing the past for what it really was. That grounds us and makes us more honest. When we are more honest we are more able to experience the real touch of God and the real movement of Holy Spirit in the world around us.*

We all know the continuum that goes all the way from "keep reality away, look back through rose-colored glasses, be afraid of what's coming" to "see the past for what it was, tell the truth about where we are, open to the movement of Spirit in our world." What ways (practices) do you have of grounding yourself in what is real *now* so that you, too, are aware of the movement of Spirit all around? What other practices might you adopt to achieve this?

C.J. talks about being Christian in his work place where he sees himself as the "quiet Christian over in the corner who's quietly going through is day," in a work environment that includes people whose Christianity is right there in front of them, highly visible. He doesn't feel compelled to announce his Christianity to the world, but in looking at the statistical charts that Diana introduced, he was struck by those who have, as part of who they are, the need to be professing their faith daily. He's left wondering where he fits in that.

His question opened an opportunity for Diana to talk about a practice that is really key in this time of change and transition—the practice of *listening*, or as many spiritual directors tend to name it, *holy listening.* Diana names and illustrates these qualities in the practice of holy listening:

- *Listening* makes a safe space for receiving other people's stories.
- *Listening* sets aside the need to be judgmental of the point-of-view of others.
- *Listening* reduces the defensiveness (and even hostility) of the other.
- *Listening* belongs to a kind of Christianity that is relaxed—receiving stories and building credibility.
- *Listening* opens a way to being able to tell our stories in a fresh and relational way.

In closing her response to C.J., Diana says:

> *That's my spirituality. That's as legitimate a spiritual place as [that of] a person who is more overt about, say, the practice of evangelism. If we thought about some of these things as spiritual as well, it would enable us to understand the beauty of this tradition as having an important place in this kind of culture.*

1. C.J. comes into this part of the conversation wondering if his way of living his Christian identity in the workplace is enough, given that other colleagues are more demonstrative in their faith witness. In response, Diana offers a reflection on listening that deeply affirms a gift that C.J. brings to others. What words (like *listening* and *evangelizing*) best describe the ways that you live your Christian identity in all the places of your life?

2. In the week ahead, find opportunities for conscious listening of the kind that Diana has described:

- Receive the other person's story or perspective without judgment, without advice, and without needing to add your own story or perspective.
- Give yourself to fully listening, setting aside the need to compose your response in your head while the other person is still speaking.
- Allow the realization to come over you that what you are doing when you listen with empathy, respect and genuineness is opening yourself and another to the Presence of God as love. This is embodied spirituality.

OPTION 5: WAKING UP TO SOULWORK
(an option for personal reflection following the session)

Following the session you will continue to think about issues raised both on the DVD and in your small group. This suggestion for journaling is offered to support you in continuing your reflection beyond the session time.

You have heard Diana talking about this as a time of *awakening* and we have explored that theme of *waking up* in a number of options for small group conversation. This is a place to think more personally about what is awakening in your life in Spirit and your participation in religious community.

Use this space and these sentence stems as a journal for written exploration of what is waking up in you:

I am waking up to…

I feel the Spirit of Life awakening in me when…

We are waking up as a community to…

CLOSING

One: Presence of Possibilities,
All: Awaken us to your creativity within.

One: Presence of Hope,
All: Awaken us to your yearning for life.

One: Presence of Love,
All: Awaken us to life lived fully in relationship.

One: Presence of Truth,
All: Awaken us to the power of our words.

One: Presence of Life emerging,
All: Awaken us to all that is becoming.

One: Presence of Blessing,
All: Be with us now and always.

Waking Up Reflection Page

> " The creed could better be rendered as, "I *belove* God, maker of heaven and earth…" Could you imagine if we just switched a couple of letters in the words *believe*–to *belove*–how that would change what happens in worship? "
>
> –*Diana Butler Bass*

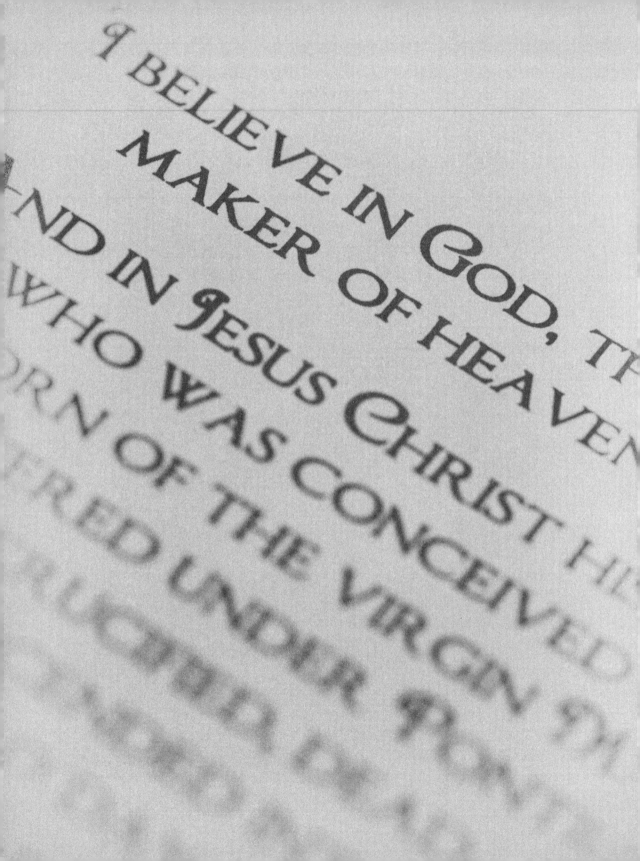

SESSION 2

Believing

BEFORE THE SESSION

Many participants like to come to the group conversation after considering individually some of the issues that will be raised. The following five reflective activities are intended to open your mind, memories and emotions regarding some aspects of this session's topic. Use the space provided here to note your reflections.

1. Diana says that the specific shape that Christianity is going to be taking in the 21st century is already with us; we can already begin to see its contours. What do you think some of those contours are?

2. Write as many responses as you can to these two questions: *What* do you believe? *How* do you believe?

3. Has someone ever asked you, "How can you possibly believe *that* when *this* is going on?" How was your relationship with belief changed as a result of that question being asked of you?

4. In this session you will hear Diana say, "If we can begin to explain how our belief changes over time, that becomes a much different engagement with people. It's not just handing them a piece of paper saying 'This is what Christians are supposed to believe,' but 'This is how I have experienced belief over my life.'" Reflect on times in your life when you actually had to speak about the dynamic of faith and belief, when you went way beyond just repeating some aspect of your church's teaching.

5. Read a favorite psalm. Whenever you come across a word for God, substitute the name *Beloved*. Notice how your relationship with God changes as you do this.

This is the second meeting of the group. There is already a sense of membership carried over from the first session; but there's a good chance there may be people attending for the first time. Make sure everyone is introduced and welcomed.

You might also take a few moments for a check-in on the theme of the session: *How Belief is Changing.* For example, each person might name one way that they live out *belief* now that is different than during an earlier time in their life. This is a quick 30-second check-in, not a time for lengthy storytelling! That will come later in the course of the session.

Play the first section of the DVD for Session 2, through Diana's presentation.

In the first part of her presentation, Diana lays out for us a framework for seeing the nature of the change that we as Christians are experiencing. She offers four key points:

1. The tradition of Christianity always changes and at times of awakening the tradition changes very rapidly and very dramatically.

2. The specific shape that Christianity is going to be taking in the 21st century is already with us. We can already begin to see its contours.

3. We're not going to a place where everything is going to be new. Human beings in the 21st century are still going to *believe*, still going to *behave* in ways related to those beliefs, and still going to have a sense of *belonging* relative to believing and behaving. We're not leaving that behind. The whole human enterprise of the "Three B's" (believing, behaving and belonging) is moving with us into the future.

4. What is changing is what the questions are under each category. During this session and the next two, we are going to examine what the questions used to be and what the questions are in the process of becoming.

In introducing herself Diana talks about her comfort with the spiritual and mystical aspect of life as well as with the scientific and academic approach to religion. How have you been involved in both of those aspects of the religious life—the spiritual and the academic? In your experience, when have you noticed that the one sustains the other?

The Three B's

BELIEVING *(understanding)*

Do you believe God exists?

BEHAVING *(action)*

Have you attended a religious service in the last week?

Belonging *(identity)*

Are you a Protestant, Catholic, Jew or other?

Diana lays out for us a powerful historical process of 500 years that has brought us to a very profound personal faith challenge for our time:

> Before the Reformation the "What do you believe?" question wasn't significant. It was assumed throughout Europe that everybody was Christian and Catholic and that everyone believed the same thing.
>
> After 1600, when there were five traditions contending for the loyalty of people, they had to be very clear about what they believed. For 200 years Christians were organizing their belief systems so that it was clear what members of various denominational loyalties believed.
>
> The answers were organized into creeds and doctrines so that if somebody asked you what you believed, you could hand them something printed from your denomination about what you believe. Our traditions are very used to responding to the "what" question.
>
> A few years ago I realized that hardly anybody in my life had been asking me the question, "What do you believe?" or "What do Christians believe?" The "what" question is almost empty space in my life. People just assume that they know what I think when they hear I'm a Christian.

> This is the way the question has changed. We've moved from the conventional question to an experiential (or spiritual) question that has to do with how we experience belief. People will ask me the question sometimes multiple times in a single day, "How do you believe that?"
>
> • "I'd be a Christian like you, but I just don't know how to believe in Jesus."
> • "I'd like to go to church but I don't know how I could ever recite the creed. How do you do that?"
> • "I don't know how to be a Christian and believe science at the same time."
> • "How in the world do you believe in the virgin-birth thing and still seem like you're a rational, intelligent and thoughtful human being in the 21st century?"

> Ultimately, people are requesting us to tell our experience of being a Christian person and how we put these pieces together in our lives—in our theological and philosophical worldviews. They are not nearly as concerned about what we believe anymore; they are asking how we believe it.

> When people used to ask what we believe, they weren't asking us personally anything; they were simply asking us for information. We could hand them something printed that was fairly objective or we could tell them to talk to a priest or minister. We didn't necessarily have to invest our own selves in the answer.

But now people are saying, "How do you do it?"

- *"How do you make sense of this story that you claim marks your life—this story about Jesus?"*
- *"How does that story connect to your life in the world?"*
- *"How do you think about science, politics and the moral life?"*

People are asking us, not just for our ideas about God, *but are asking us to give them our story* about the convictions that form our lives. *That can be very intimidating for people to engage in.*

This is a huge switch.

This is the new question.

This has become the primary faith question in our time.

1. What experience have you had personally of the kind of challenge that Diana is describing, namely, being required to speak about the convictions that form your life, not just your ideas about God as expressed in such things as creeds and church teachings?

2. Diana suggests that this requirement to be more personal in speaking of one's faith can be intimidating for people. What feelings and/or thoughts do you have about it?

OPTIONS FOR FURTHER EXPLORATION

Before going on to choose from the following options for conversation and reflection, watch the second section of the DVD for Session 2, in which Diana continues to teach, but in the context of her conversation with members of the group.

OPTION 1: ON HOW TO LIVE THE EXPERIENCE OF BELIEF

The conversation that follows and that you have heard on the DVD leads us into profound reflection on the changing nature of belief that Diana has been addressing. Read the conversation and the affirmations that accompany it, then spend time on the reflective questions that follow, which are intended to stimulate similar conversation in your group.

C.J. says:

When I was faced with answering the "how" question after my wife passed away and my kids asked me directly, "Dad, how can you go to church, how can you pray? Where was God in this?" I have to admit that I had never come to grips with an answer that I felt was satisfactory. The "how" gets into my gut and bothers me because I'm not sure I have an answer and I don't know what to say.

Affirmation 1:

There are times when we cannot answer the questions that seem to lie at the very heart of our faith.

Diana says:

After the children were shot at the school in Newtown, Connecticut, I was on the phone with my best friend who happens to be an atheist. We were talking about the memorial service that was televised and she said to me, "You see, it's things like this that I don't know how it is you can be a Christian. I mean this kind of evil and the answers that I'm hearing from religious people in the world. This makes no sense to me. How does your faith account for the murder of these children?"

I feel that I'm pretty able to deal with "how" questions. I'm pretty intentional about thinking in this way. When she said that, I was literally silenced because she said it in such a forceful way. I just confessed to her, "You know, I don't know how, and I have to say I'm pretty upset about this." She replied, "That's actually all I need to hear you say. I don't want to hear the easy answers coming from Christians on this one. I want to hear you say that you don't know how."

Affirmation 2:

Speaking the truth about our inability to come up with answers is not only the only thing to do, it is the very best thing to do.

Diana continues:

She led me to a place to understand my own doubt, which is part of our spiritual lives. I think that the moment that we don't know what to say is the moment we have encountered the "how" questions in a deep sense and that becomes holy ground for being with people or for looking at what it is going to mean to be Christian in the 21st century when we will increasingly be encountered by these how questions.

Affirmation 3:

Sharing our vulnerability creates a holy ground where relationships can be formed and deepened.

Marilyn observes:

> The "how" changes. It changes with just living. It changes with our experiences. It changes with time. There were two times when I thought I knew the "how," and then something impossible happened. First, my husband died. I had gone through all the stages of adjusting—his illness—his dying—and I was living in a place I never thought I would be, living like I thought I would never live and experiencing growth of the "how" in ways that I didn't think it could grow. I became comfortable with that "how."

Affirmation 4:

Life circumstances will constantly offer challenges to the stability of belief we thought would stay forever.

Marilyn continues:

> Then all of a sudden I found that my kidney was dead and I was going to be a kidney dialysis patient for as long as that would last, which could be three or four years. So now it's the "how" to prepare for the reality that I might be dying. And then I thought that a lot of the restraints I had on my life didn't need to be there anymore,e because I wouldn't really be here that long. I didn't have to think in terms of 20 more years of life. Many of the ways I thought I had to behave I really didn't have to. It freed me to feel ways that I didn't think I could feel.

> Then I got a transplant. So now I had to pull back thinking that I was going to be here for 20 more years. I had to make more adjustments in my thinking. The "how" developed and with it growth I didn't think I would have to face. It all goes back to what my mother said, "Just keep living and what you don't understand, you may develop a way to understand it or you may develop a way to live so that you don't have to understand everything. Put it in the hands of God. God knows."

Affirmation 5:

We are saved by our capacity for growth in understanding and in our willingness not to have all the answers.

Diana responds:

That's a beautiful testimony to the experience of belief. What I'm talking about is what it is to experience belief not just be able to have a piece of paper so you can give the same answers over and over again. When we think about formalized creeds or doctrines, there's a very real way in which people in the larger cultural context— for example, when we say we believe in Jesus— think of it as a flat creedal statement. If we can begin to explain how our belief changes over time, that becomes a much different engagement with people. It's not just handing them a piece of paper saying this is what Christians are supposed to believe, but this is how I have experienced belief over my life.

Affirmation 6:

We will find increasing opportunity to speak openly about the dynamic, ever-changing reality of our faith life. It will matter that we speak.

---

1. As you read this conversation and the affirmations, where do you find it touching on the experience of your own journey of faith?

2. What new options do you see for yourself after hearing the stories and reflections offered here? If possible, speak about specific situations in your own life.

Diana takes time to introduce us to a more accurate sense of our key word in this session: *belief* and *believing*:

> *The word* belief *is a very strange word in English. When you look at the New Testament, the word for believe in Greek is the word* pistis *or* pisteuo *which means "to trust" or "to faith." There's really no verb in English that means "to faith," so when the Bible was being translated from Greek into English in the 16th and 17th centuries, translators really struggled with how to take the Greek* pisteuo *meaning "to faith" and put it in English. They came across the word* believe, *which in their context did not mean to have ideas or opinions about something. It meant "to belove"—to be devoted to something or to trust something.*

> *So the word* believe *actually holds within its roots this very experiential kind of dimension of "how." Believing isn't about signing your name on the dotted line consenting to a group of ideas or having opinions about God. It's literally our disposition toward that God. In fact the creed could better be rendered as, "I belove God, maker of heaven and earth…" Could you imagine if we just switched a couple of letters in the word* believe—*to belove—how that would change what happens in worship?*

Sharon picks up this sense of belief by reflecting on the way that spiritual practice shapes her disposition toward the holy—her *beloving* of God:

> *I've been listening to you all and not thinking so much about events in my life but about intentional spiritual practice. That's how I believe. I'm a spiritual practice enthusiast. I try lots of different things. I love practices from icon work to meditation, from different types of prayer to reading scripture. That shows me how to believe. It forms me and shapes me. These are times I cherish.*

1. What difference would it make to you if you were to say or think "belove" whenever the word *believe* was given by the text (for example in saying the creed)?

2. What difference does it make to think of God as your Beloved rather than the one in whom you believe? Take a favorite psalm and whenever you come across a word for God, substitute the word *Beloved*.

3. What spiritual practices deepen your relationship with the Beloved?

OPTION 3: JUST WHEN I THOUGHT I HAD IT ALL FIGURED OUT...
(an option for personal reflection following the session)

Following the session you will continue to think about issues raised both on the DVD and in your small group. This suggestion for journaling is offered to support you in continuing your reflection beyond the session time.

These are the six affirmation statements from Option 1, changed to make them more personal to you. Choose one or more of them and use it as a starting point either for a journal reflection or for a conversation with a friend over your favorite beverage.

- There are times when I cannot answer the questions that seem to lie at the very heart of my faith.

- Speaking the truth about my inability to come up with answers is not only the only thing to do, it is the very best thing to do.

- Sharing my vulnerability creates a holy ground where my relationships can be formed and deepened.

- Life circumstances will constantly offer challenges to the stability of belief I thought would stay forever.

- I am saved by my capacity for growth in understanding and in my willingness not to have all the answers.

- I will find increasing opportunity to speak openly about the dynamic, ever-changing reality of my faith life. It will matter that I speak.

One: Presence of Possibilities,
All: Beloved, Spirit Within.

One: Presence of Hope,
All: Beloved, Eternal Now.

One: Presence of Compassion,
All: Beloved, Heart of our Hearts.

One: Presence of Truth,
All: Beloved, Source of all Courage.

One: Presence of Life emerging,
All: Beloved, Our Holy Ground.

One: Presence of Blessing,
All: Belove us now and always. *Amen.*

BELIEVING REFLECTION PAGE

> " One of the things I love about the lives of the saints is that hardly any of them followed the rules. They all departed from what the rules of their own time were, in their pursuit of the radical practice of the life of Jesus in their world. "
>
> *—Diana Butler Bass*

SESSION | 3

BEHAVING

Many participants like to come to the group conversation after considering individually some of the issues that will be raised. The following five reflective activities are intended to open your mind, memories and emotions regarding some aspects of this session's topic. Use the space provided here to note your reflections.

1. As you anticipate this next session, assess the life of your congregation along this continuum:

■——□

a conventional church focused
on lists of do's and don'ts that
just don't connect to the questions
of existence today

a community of faith that models
practices that enable its members
to live with meaning and purpose
in a rapidly changing world

2. One of the participants in this week's session talks about his life with God as "untidy." What words would you use to describe your life with God?

3. In this session you will hear Diana say, "The people who embody hospitality in heroic fashion become the saints." Go to the website of the Episcopal Church of St. Gregory of Nyssa in San Francisco (www.allsaintscompany.org/dancing-saints-all-icons) to see all the people that congregation recognizes as saints *(All Saints Company: Drawing from Fresh and Ancient Springs)*. Whom would you include in your "wall of saints"?

4. What is it about your membership in a community of faith that makes the challenging life of being a follower of Jesus less intimidating and perhaps to be deeply desired?

5. In the days before this next session pay attention for times when you face a choice or a place where you can take an initiative (or not). The question that confronts you is, "What am I going to do?" Notice how you go about making that decision: the influences and factors, your own internal process, the level of risk, and so on.

This is the third meeting of the group. Included in this session is an emphasis on the practice of hospitality.

How does this group express hospitality to its members...
- by providing gifts of refreshment?
- by ensuring that everyone is comfortable?
- by making sure that everyone's name is known?
- by providing space for people to check in about matters of concern and celebration?
- by being clear about who will carry primary responsibility for the facilitation of the session?

Notice how every group of which you are a part develops its own practices of hospitality both consciously and by default. We are naturally hospitable beings; but even so we can miss out on the most obvious opportunities for expressing welcome and acknowledgement.

ESSENTIAL: THE "BEHAVING" QUESTION IS CHANGING TOO

Play the first section of the DVD for Session 3, through Diana's presentation.

Here is a summary of what you just heard Diana address on the DVD:

	Before	**Now**
The Question	How do you do that?	What are we going to do?
Assumption behind the Question	If you could just come up with the right set of rules you could fix all the things that are disordered and broken.	There is no one set of rules that could be applied to the world as it is now; every situation is different.
Action that Follows	Find the rules and techniques to apply.	Open the imagination to engage the "What are we going to do?" question.
In the Spirit of...	order	discernment
Leads to...	a conventional church focused on lists of do's and don'ts that fail to connect to the questions of existence today.	practices for individuals and communities that enable us to live with meaning and purpose in a rapidly changing world.

1. Where does Diana's presentation connect with your lived experience in a church community and organization?

2. For some folks, it takes a lot of courage to even imagine moving from the question as it was *(How do you do that?)* to the question as it is becoming *(What are we going to do?)*. What is your emotional response to the call to move even more boldly away from rules and techniques and toward practices and discernment?

OPTIONS FOR FURTHER EXPLORATION

Before going on to choose from the following options for conversation and reflection, watch the second portion of the DVD for Session 3, in which Diana continues to teach, but in the context of her conversation with members of the group.

OPTION 1: REQUIREMENTS, SUGGESTIONS OR A THIRD WAY?

Alex asks this question:

Diana, do you think that the church is putting out a message that says, "If you want to be in this faith you have *to do these things…," or a message that says, "If you want to be part of this, we* suggest *that you do these things…"? Is the list of rules put there as* requirements *or* suggestions?

As you have heard, Diana offers a *third* way in her response:

What I am offering here is that we take away the language or rules completely and instead think about congregations as communities of practice.

A community of practice…
- sees that there are particular ways of behaving that are meaningful in relationship to scripture, the life of God in the world and the person of Jesus;
- provides a setting in which its members learn about key practices such as true hospitality and moves deeper into living these practices;
- moves away from the language of rules toward a language of sharing, teaching, learning and mentoring.

Talk together about times when you have actually lived the vision that Diana is articulating here. When were you a member of a *community of practice* that followed these three definitional statements? How did that grow you?

OPTION 2: THE UNTIDY LIFE WITH GOD

C.J. opens up this consideration:

Having rules can make life easier because you don't have to make choices; however, if there are rules that make you part of the group and define who you are, then it takes all the pleasure out of being able to think and to be creative. I find it hard in my own religious and spiritual journey to think that God laid these rules down as if there were only one way to do anything. It's so much more personal when you can work as a partner in that relationship. A rule-laden relationship with God doesn't allow for a personal relationship. I prefer to have conversations with God about where I am and what's going on. If I can break out of the rules and traditions that keep me bound, then life is way more enriching and expansive. Life isn't neat and tidy, and life with God isn't neat and tidy either.

What do you make of C.J.'s theology? Describe times in your life when you were relieved to have something like a rule or a tradition to hold on to. Then consider other times in your life when you thrived on the opportunity to work out with God the way to go forward. Share these recollections with each other. Where and how do your experiences mesh? Where and how do they differ?

The group engages in conversation about the challenges of living out the practice of true hospitality. In response to their concerns Diana offers these thoughts:

Notice that as soon as you start talking about hospitality, there's no simple rule for doing it—how often you let a stranger in the door or how often you drop a dollar in a stranger's hat. The question becomes, "What am I going to do in this particular situation?" Thus it becomes an issue of discernment.

You have to bring to bear your experience as a Christian person to answer the questions. There's no rule.

There is a cultural standard of hospitality which is somewhat corrupted, but then there's the gospel and the overall witness of the Christian tradition with their standard of hospitality which can be pretty risky.

These practices of hospitality are quite radical and can be interpreted in radical ways. The people who embody hospitality in heroic fashion became the saints. They become our models of excellence that we are supposed to pursue.

One of the things I love about the lives of the saints is that hardly any of them followed the rules! They all departed from what the rules of their own time were, in their pursuit of the radical practice of the life of Jesus in the world.

There's a great story from the early 4th century church about the traveler, Rufinus, who after walking through the Egyptian desert for many hours, came with his friends to a monastery. The monks, upon seeing the travelers approaching, didn't wait for them to come to the door, but ran out to the road and brought them gifts of wine, honey and water. After offering them nourishment right there on the road, they washed their feet and brought them in. These kinds of stories have to be constantly in our imaginations.

1. What challenges have you experienced in living out "gospel" hospitality? What wisdom do you now carry and offer as a result of those challenges?

3. When you hear the story of Rufinus and the monks, what is stirred in you?

2. What does it take to be a saint? To what extent to you aspire to sainthood?

In response to C.J.'s exclamation, "It ain't easy being Christian!" Diana offers some reflections on the blessing of living the challenges of the way of Jesus in community:

- Together we hold one another to that life of increasing practice. We are not alone.

- It's true that it's not easy, but there is something that happens when we're together and you can admit to a friend that you have failed at something, and your friend offers you forgiveness: "Maybe you can do better next time; and I still love you anyway."

- The togetherness as a community of practice actually aids in that hard way of life and makes it easier to bear.

- We could do practice in isolation, but then we just wind up frustrated and feeling like it's too hard. If we do it together, we get let off the hook at the right times and we get our feet held to the fire at the right times.

Go around the circle and name times when you each experienced how membership in a community of practice made a difference for you in living this way of being in the world.

OPTION 5: WHAT AM I GOING TO DO NOW?
(an option for personal reflection following the session)

Following the session you will continue to think about issues raised both on the DVD and in your small group. This suggestion for journaling is offered to support you in continuing your reflection beyond the session time.

Diana has been clear with us that the question of "Behaving" has changed from "How are we going to do that?" to "What are we going to do now?" We have observed in our conversation the importance of struggling to discern the best "in the moment" response to the question, rather than falling back on a rule or a traditional response to tell us what to do.

- During the days ahead, carry very consciously the question, "What am I going to do now?"

- Notice situations where that question is alive for you: "What am I going to do now?"

- Witness yourself as a faithful person discerning a response: "What am I going to do now?"

- Notice that even when you don't think there is an issue at hand, just to ask the question changes the circumstances in which you find yourself: "What am I going to do now?"

You have choices about how to process these experiences. Personal writing or artistic reflection is a more introverted style; whereas meeting with a friend for conversation feeds the extraverted preference. You are both introvert and extravert, but with a preference. Choose thoughtfully how to proceed. What are you going to do now?

CLOSING

One: Presence of Possibilities,
All: Accompany us in our choosing.

One: Presence of Inspiration,
All: Enthuse us in our living.

One: Presence of Hospitality,
All: Embolden us in our attending.

One: Presence of Spontaneity,
All: Surprise us in our forgetting.

One: Presence of Chaos,
All: Ground us in our struggling.

One: Presence of Requirement,
All: Accompany us in our faithing.

One: Presence of Blessing,
All: Love us in our Being, now and always. *Amen.*

> " People are creating new kinds of communities. These communities are very powerful in creating self-identity, but they are different from the traditional kind of labeled communities that we know. "
>
> —*Diana Butler Bass*

SESSION | 4

BELONGING

BEFORE THE SESSION

Many participants like to come to the group conversation after considering individually some of the issues that will be raised. The following five reflective activities are intended to open your mind, memories and emotions regarding some aspects of this session's topic. Use the space provided here to note your reflections.

1. The first section of the study, "Essential: A New Question of Belonging" (p. 65), provides a format for you to do some reflection ahead of the session. In the DVD you will hear Diana introduce this matter of belonging at greater length. By taking time to follow the process in "Essential: A New Question of Belonging," you will be prepared to bring more personal reflection to your participation in the session.

2. Make a date for a conversation with someone of an older generation than yours. Your task is to uncover differences in the level of acceptance of religious and spiritual diversity over the last few generations. What specific stories can you find that illustrate the degree of change? How is this change in acceptance also changing the nature of relationship and community?

3. Read this passage from Paul's letter to the small Christian community in Corinth:

I have a serious concern to bring up with you, my friends, using the authority of Jesus, our Master. I'll put it as urgently as I can: You must get along with each other. You must learn to be considerate of one another, cultivating a life in common.

I bring this up because some from Chloe's family brought a most disturbing report to my attention—that you're fighting among yourselves! I'll tell you exactly what I was told: You're all picking sides, going around saying, "I'm on Paul's side," or "I'm for Apollos," or "Peter is my man," or "I'm in the Messiah group." I ask you, "Has the Messiah been chopped up in little pieces so we can each have a relic all our own?

— 1 Corinthians 1:10-13a, *The Message*

At the heart of this passage is the question, "Whose are you?" How do you live this question in the life of your faith community where relationship has at least two expressions: one with Christ/God and one with your friends?

4. Archbishop Desmond Tutu says this about the South African concept of *Ubuntu*:

> *It means my humanity is caught up, is inextricably bound up, in theirs. We belong in a bundle of life. We say, "A person is a person through other people." It is not "I think therefore I am." It says rather: "I am human because I belong." I participate, I share.*
> —www.walkoutwalkon.net/south-africa/ubuntu-i-am-because-you-are/

In your journal or in your daily time of reflection, consider the depth of the Archbishop's wisdom as expressed in the African concept of *Ubuntu*.

5. Diana says in this session: "Our lives exist in a nexus of relationships in and through community. When we talk about ourselves, we have to take into account this complex network. Our identity has become profoundly relational." How would you give expression to that network visually (drawing, painting, digitally, with clay and so on)? Try it. What do you notice?

This fourth session of *Embracing Spiritual Awakening* is all about *belonging*. In the course of the session you will think and talk together about ways that you and other people talk about *belonging* in a religious and spiritual sense. It's all about *identity*.

As a way of bringing the members of the group back together and plunging into the theme of this session, go around the circle asking each person to complete the "I am _____" stem, with words that describe their spiritual and religious identity today.

Some of you might just say "I am *Episcopalian* (or *Presbyterian, Methodist, Baptist*, etc.)" and feel that that's enough. Some of you may want to say more than that.

Observe the uniqueness of each person's response.

ESSENTIAL: A NEW QUESTION OF BELONGING

Play the first section of the DVD for Session 4, through Diana's presentation.

For a long time the "Belonging" Question has been:

Who are you?

When you were a younger adult (or teenager) and someone asked you, "Who are you?" how did you respond? When asked about your *religious identity*, how did you typically respond?

I am...

Have you ever announced your identity in that way? What would you likely say if you found that a single word label was no longer adequate?

I am...

When did identity shift from being a single word to a paragraph? What's going on?
- The old labels no longer encompass the reality of our being in the world.
- Now we need to identify ourselves in relationship to a whole range of things.
- Our lives exist in a nexus of relationships in and through community.
- When we talk about ourselves we have to take into account this complex network.
- Our identity has become profoundly relational.
- We have shifted from an emphasis on membership to more personal constructs.

Up to a few decades ago, most people tended to answer the question with a label that reflected membership in a church, synagogue, temple or other religious gathering place, for example, *I am an Episcopalian, Catholic, Jew, Presbyterian, Muslim,* and so on.

But now labels seem to be an inadequate way of describing who we are. Our identity is shifting, but so is the way that we announce our identity: *I am a spiritual person who happens to go to a Presbyterian Church...where we engage in meaningful practices of faith...and embody justice in the world.*

The belonging question has shifted from *Who are you?* to:

Whose are you?

Where have you been aware in your own church and community of the reality of what Diana is presenting here, this shift in the way we talk about our religious identity?

OPTIONS FOR FURTHER EXPLORATION

Before going on to choose from the following options for conversation and reflection, watch the second section of the DVD for Session 4, in which Diana continues to teach, but in the context of her conversation with members of the group.

OPTION 1: WHOSE ARE YOU?

Diana tells us about the personal transformation that happened in her first teaching job in a very conservative evangelical college in Southern California. Her task was to teach a required course in Christian doctrine to large classes of 18-year-old evangelicals. Furthermore, she was expected to teach it so that they would actually live out the doctrine as good evangelicals in the world. The conversation in the classroom went something like this:

Diana: Evangelicals believe that…

Student: What's an evangelical?

Diana: You are! Didn't you read the statement of faith you signed in your application to be here?

Student: Well, I'm just a Christian.

Diana: But that's so vague. Why are you here?

Student: Because my friend is here.

Diana began to see that, for many students, their identity was not based on the evangelical party platform that she had constructed in her mind as a young baby-boomer thinking in traditional concepts of believing, behaving and belonging. In fact they had come there as Christians who loved Jesus and who wanted to be in the same college as their friends. They had a very profound sense of who they were, and it was different from Diana's construction of their identity and belonging. Diana began to see, thanks to these students, that there was a shift underway that was showing up in generational differences.

Marilyn connects Diana's narrative back to the conversation from an earlier session where we had seen the statistical shift in religious affiliation:

> When we look back at your charts we can see that those people you refer to as "unaffiliated" are actually being affiliated by their friends. They're not really looking at the labels we're using to describe why they're where they are.

Diana responds:

People are creating new kinds of communities. Those communities are very powerful in creating self-identity, but they are different from the traditional kind of labeled communities that we know. This makes it kind of scary for people in the traditional communities who would like their kids to become, for example, Roman Catholic. Their children and grandchildren are making communities in new ways. How do we get those kinds of communities and traditional religious communities in conversation with one another?

Marilyn observes:

In our hospitality, we—the older people—have to listen to what the younger people are saying so that we can understand what they're doing, so that we don't try to make them fit the labels we think they ought to fit.

1. What experience do you have of people "affiliating" in new ways?

2. What new kinds of religious "belonging" are you witnessing in the cultural landscape of North America?

When Diana asks Alex about his experience of high school as a place where he can feel free to be who he really is, he responds:

> One of the things that bothers me about my large, high-school cafeteria is that groups are separated by race. However, the thing I never see is separation by religion. One of my best friends is an atheist and the other is a Jew. I can't recall a time when there's been some sort of issue that, because we belong to different traditions, there's been anything keeping us from getting to know one another. It seems good to me that, although we can all claim to belong somewhere, we can all still be around other people who don't belong where we belong.

Diana responds:

> You and your two best friends belong to one another and you've made a friendship be primary. Not so long ago an atheist, a Jew and a Christian would have been separated by their identities. The labels of your religious identification are secondary to this relational friendship that you've formed. The labels of religion are breaking down more quickly and we're able to live in a much more pluralistic religious environment. We're about fifteen years behind when it comes to racial pluralism. We're now able to cross religious boundaries that would not so long ago have segregated people.

Diana shares with us the story of her mother, a Methodist, not being able to be in the wedding party of her best friend, a Catholic. She concludes:

> Not so long ago in America, it would have been impossible for you and your two best friends to get along. We've moved in a completely different direction in jumping over these old religious boundaries. Alex, your story is really rich in showing how we've shaped as a nation and where we still need to be challenged to change.

Sharon then tells us this delightful story of spirited creativity in the face of religious zeal that underscores again how times have changed in the religious culture of North America:

> My husband is Jewish, a para-rabbi in the Reform Jewish Tradition. When we got married we went to the Rabbi, and I had to take a course in how to be Jewish. We had to promise that our children would be Jewish. Then I went to the Episcopal priest who required that my husband take communion at the wedding since he had previously been baptized and then had converted to Judaism. We also had to promise that our children would be Episcopalian! So with good faith we promised that we would raise our children Jewish and we would raise our children Episcopalian. And we did!

1. What stories do you have that confirm this trend in significant cultural change that Alex, Sharon and Diana are identifying?

2. Why do you think there's a more dramatic change in the pace of *religious* integration than in *racial* integration? When, if ever, have you noticed in yourself a tendency toward more acceptance of religious difference than racial diversity?

Diana tells us:

There's an important passage in the New Testament where Paul is talking to a quarreling Corinthian Church where people are arguing over whose they are:

> I have a serious concern to bring up with you, my friends, using the authority of Jesus, our Master. I'll put it as urgently as I can: You *must* get along with each other. You must learn to be considerate of one another, cultivating a life in common.
>
> I bring this up because some from Chloe's family brought a most disturbing report to my attention—that you're fighting among yourselves! I'll tell you exactly what I was told: You're all picking sides, going around saying, "I'm on Paul's side," or "I'm for Apollos," or "Peter is my man," or "I'm in the Messiah group." I ask you, "Has the Messiah been chopped up in little pieces so we can each have a relic all our own?"
>
> — 1 Corinthians 1:10-13a,
> *The Message*

In the letter, Paul says that the truth of it is that we all belong to Christ.

We also do our belonging in the context of human relationship. What happened in Corinthians is a human thing; we belong to these different people whom we are connected to, whose words, beliefs and passions we find meaningful too. These two levels of belonging are always functioning: the broad more spiritual tradition (we are God's, we are Jesus') as well as the human one (we are one another's).

It's interesting to me that the Diocese of Virginia this past few weeks has been having a little dust-up about the limits of belonging. The "dust-up" came when the bishop permitted a more controversial speaker than some to come in and do an officially sanctioned event. There was a group of people who protested and said that it was inappropriate and he should not be given the sanction of the Episcopal Church. They were saying, in effect, that there was a limit on what the identity of this particular group of people should be. It was a beautiful thing when the bishop wrote back and said that we are a community where we all belong to one another. It's not a community that's isolating itself from people who have worthwhile and interesting things to say and new perspectives to offer us. The bishop was, in effect, saying that we're going to be a community where all belonging is welcomed.

We did the same thing, of course, with the blessing of same sex unions—opening the door and saying that we're going to be a community where we're allowing the possibility of a big range of relationships that will inevitably challenge us in some cases. By being related to this wide variety of people we become more ourselves. It reminds me of what Desmond Tutu said, "I am because you are." We exist because we all exist. That relate-ability is the fundamental point of human identity.

Speak about times when living the full range of human experience in community—even when challenging for you—has opened you to more of who you really are in your God-alive identity.

OPTION 4: LIVING THE QUESTIONS
(an option for personal reflection following the session)

Following the session, you will continue to think about issues raised both on the DVD and in your small group. This suggestion for journaling is offered to support you in continuing your reflection beyond the session time.

We are never done with the basic questions of identity! Diana has offered us two key questions of identity: *Who am I?* and *Whose am I?*

Continue to live out the difference in these two questions in this way:
- Ask a friend to sit with you with pen and paper.
- At the top of one page have them write the question, "Who are you?"
- They are to keep asking you the question for 5 minutes—"Who are you? Who are you?"—as you continue to offer responses.
- They are to record in list form all your responses.
- No other conversation is allowed.
- Keep going for the 5 minutes, even if you think you have run out of responses.

Now repeat the process with the other question: "Whose are you?"
- At the top of a second page have them write the question, "Whose are you?"
- They are to keep asking you the question for five minutes—"Whose are you? Whose are you?"—as you continue to offer responses.
- Once again they are to record in list form all your responses.
- No other conversation is allowed.
- Keep going for the 5 minutes, even if you think you have run out of responses.

Now look at both lists of responses. What do you notice? Share insights with your friend. Now repeat the activity while you ask your friend the questions and record his/her answers.

CLOSING

One: Presence of Possibilities,
All: We are because You are.

One: Presence of Belonging,
All: We are because You are.

One: Presence of Meaning,
All: We are because You are.

One: Presence of Relationship,
All: We are because You are.

One: Presence of Memory,
All: We are because You are.

One: Presence of Unfolding,
All: We are because You are.

One: Presence of Blessing,
All: We are because You are, now and always. *Amen.*

BELONGING REFLECTION PAGE

" That's the great thing about awakenings: they never are what we think they are going to be... "

–*Diana Butler Bass*

SESSION | 5

AWAKENING

BEFORE THE SESSION

Many participants like to come to the group conversation after considering individually some of the issues that will be raised. The following five reflective activities are intended to open your mind, memories and emotions regarding some aspects of this session's topic. Use the space provided here to note your reflections.

1. In anticipation of seeing the DVD of Diana teaching in this session, go to ESSENTIAL 1 (p. 84) and work your way through the three questions at the end of this section.

2. Up to now we have been thinking of the three B's in this order: *believe, behave* and *belong*. What difference does it make in you when you reverse the order and make belonging the starting point for contemporary faith? (See the notes in ESSENTIAL 2, p. 86.)

3. Take time to reflect on the ways that you enliven your faith through experience. How do you do that? What part does music play in the experiencing of your spirituality and faith? Have you ever been on a pilgrimage? What kind of liturgical practice touches you most deeply? What kind of contemplative experiences (like Taize chanting, centering prayer and silent retreats) have deepened your experience of the holy and renewed your spirit for action in the world?

4. Read the text in OPTION 2 (p. 89), noting especially the seven underlined statements. Which of those especially ring true for you as you think about where we are heading in this time of dramatic re-awakening.

5. Take time to go back over the study guide for the four previous sessions as well as any notes you may have made. This is a time to be bringing it all together and integrating your insights. What have you learned that you want to be sure to remember? What do you want to say to the other people in your small group as part of the closing session? Is there anything you want to ask Diana or say to her as part of your closing this learning experience?

This is the final meeting of the group. Rather than thinking about building your learning community, you are naturally thinking about ending it and reflecting with gratitude on what it has meant for you all to be together in these five sessions. And so we end on the theme of *awakening:*

- When we come together in small study groups and focus on the real stuff of our lives, *we awaken.*

- When we share a keen anticipation of the time we will spend together in holy conversation, *we awaken.*

- When we engage with innovative and provocative ideas in the safety of an intentional learning group, *we awaken.*

- When we accompany one another in the reconfiguring of our familiar frameworks of meaning, *we awaken.*

- When we carry significance in one another's lives in the days between our meetings, *we awaken.*

- When we anticipate and initiate future learning opportunities in community, *we awaken.*

Be sure to leave time later in the session for closing words of acknowledgement and appreciation.

Play the first section of the DVD for Session 5, through the end of Diana's presentation. Note that while Diana is teaching, she will refer to the chart on page 85, "From Institution to Experience." Have this page ready for quick reference.

As this session begins, Diana returns to the key word of session 1: *Awakening*.

Awakening is about…

… a reshaping of faith and theological questions.

… a deeper engagement of Christian people in the world.

… waking up to where the Spirit is pushing and pulling us to do the work of God in the world.

… an encounter with God anew that allows our lives, our communities and our world to change.

Awakening is *not* about numbers, although times of awakening typically result in an increase in church membership.

In short, awakening is about *transformation*. Refer again to the chart on page 85, "From Institution to Experience."

Focus 1: From Dogma to Conviction

When we talk about *how* we believe, rather than *what* we believe, we are in the territory of conviction. "I believe in…" becomes "I am convicted that…"

What *awakens* in you when you move from the language of *belief* to the language of *conviction?*

Focus 2: From Rules to Practices

Rules don't completely go away; what goes away is making the rules into a god. That's what practice is like in the Christian life. When we are younger, we learn the rules, but as we practice, the rules lessen in significance and the creative process of what it means to be a Christian opens up.

What *awakens* in you when you move from the language of rules to the language of practices?

Focus 3: From Members to Neighbors

There is no meatier question in the New Testament than when we get asked, "Who is your neighbor?" In the 21st century our identity is being re-shaped by a world where everyone is our neighbor. We also know that we live in a divinely constituted neighborhood and that God is part of the equation.

We are with, in, through and because of God.

We are with, in, through and because of one another.

We are profoundly aware of how our identity is shaped *by being connected in both of these realities.*

What *awakens* in you when move from the language of *member* to the language of *neighbor?*

From Institution to Experience

	Religion	Spirituality
Believing	*What:* Dogma Ideas and opinions about God	*How:* Conviction Understandings of God through an encounter in the context of life experience
Behaving	*How:* Rules Programs with specific goals that guarantee results	*What:* Practices Practices that draw participants into crafting a way of life
Belonging	*Who:* Members Propositional identity, personhood is based on extrinsic sources of inheritance, status or choice. Members submit to the authority of others.	*Whose:* Neighbors Prepositional identity, personhood is inherently linked with relationships, networks and communities. Neighbors claim agency over the direction of the future.

The palette of questions that we have explored in these four previous sessions is what many people are saying is the emerging shape of 21st century Christianity. Our theology, our worship life, our understanding of mission and justice are being re-imagined through this set of questions. But there's *one last thing* that needs to be done with the questions.

When we were growing up, we used to begin our faith life with "What do you believe?" (BELIEVE), then "How do you do it?" (BEHAVE) and finally "Who am I?" (BELONG).

Now we are reversing the order in which we address these three.

The locus of our spiritual lives is "Who are we with?" (not "What do you believe?"). The questions now come in this order:

1. BELONG—NEIGHBORS

Contemporary faith is being rearranged by our relationships with others and the communities in which we find ourselves.

We are figuring out new ways of acting together.

2. BEHAVE—PRACTICES

In making meaning in our lives, what's emerging are new understandings of God— new ways of conceptualizing what this beautiful universe is about.

3. BELIEVE—CONVICTIONS

We are really going through a process of coming to new belief, new conviction, through each other and our practices.

This is the map of awakening!

We are asking new questions, *but we are also putting those questions in a different order than our ancestors did.* In doing that, we will continue to be Christian people, followers of Jesus, but it's going to be understood in a different way than what people understood Christianity to be a generation or two ago.

Awakening is more than adding bodies to church buildings.

Awakening is a deep transformation of faith that gives us the ability to see God and our neighbors in new ways. Once your eyes are opened you begin to see it everywhere.

Diana is convinced that we are going through a great awakening in our own time.

1. In what ways does this reversal of the order of the three B's ring true for you in your experience?

2. What are the implications for you personally of this new map of awakening?

OPTIONS FOR FURTHER EXPLORATION

Before going on to choose from the following options for conversation and reflection, watch the second section of the DVD for Session 5, in which Diana continues to teach, but in the context of her conversation with members of the group.

OPTION 1: AWAKENING TO EXPERIENTIAL FAITH

Greg responds to Diana:

I like that the word awakening *has been reclaimed in a positive light. I'm definitely one who is scared of the word* revival *and even* awakening. *From these sessions I feel affirmed that community can be the initial driving force of religion or faith. I like the sense of reclaiming that; it's positive. I was afraid of losing a semblance of the Episcopal tradition that I've grown up with. Pentecostalism just isn't for me! Turns out we're already a part of it; it's just not what we thought awakening was.*

Diana adds:

That's the great thing about awakenings: they never are what we think they're going to be in advance. Pentecostalism is only one form of experiential religion in the 21st century. What we're talking about here is experiential faith—how that becomes meaningful and personal for an entirely new set of beings on the planet.

Experiential faith is manifesting itself in things as diverse as Pentecostalism, Taize chant, Celtic spirituality and pilgrimage.

The impulse is shared but the embodiment of it is taking a lot of different forms:
- from throwing your arms up in worship to participating in contemplative prayer;
- from going with a small group on a pilgrimage on the Camino to sitting around in a living room with a small group doing an experiential Bible study;
- from attending a worship in a beautiful church with a rich tradition of music like St. Paul's to sitting around playing guitar with friends.

It's not what you're doing per se; it's the disposition of experiential faith that is filling these multitudes of forms of faith that we have, and that appeal to us in many ways because we're all different human beings. When we awaken and we reconnect to God and the universe, that can happen through a beautiful 16th century piece of music or through singing a praise chorus. That's part of the beautiful diversity of human community.

How is the universal impulse toward experiential faith showing up in diverse forms in your life and in the life of your faith community?

OPTION 2: HAVING A GOOD TIME MAKING THE FUTURE

Listening to Diana's teaching, C.J. has been moved to think about the matter of our orientation toward past and future:

> I've always felt that what was past was useful and helpful, but if we're so grounded in it that we want to cling to what was, you never see what can be and where you're going. Diana, you use the word emerging *in relation to church. I want a willingness to accept the emerging feeling within (1)* and not be holding on to the past. I'm not living thousands of years ago. I'm living in 2013. When I open my eyes I'm looking to apply this teaching to the world I'm in. I've worked with folks on the caboose of the train who can see where we've been, but you're in the cab and can see where we're going. *It's okay if we're not following the same path we have been following. It's kind of liberating (2).*

Alex, by far the youngest member of the group, picks up on C.J.'s reflection:

> I'm curious to see where it's going to go—to see what it will become and what it will be like. Most of you have talked about how things have changed. *I'm interested to see how it's going to change again (3)* because it hasn't changed much since I've been alive. I'm interested to see where it's going to take me. I'm not saying that I'm going to let it take me wherever it goes. *I want it to take me if it's something good and it turns out to be something very meaningful in my life (4).* I'd really like to see how it turns out.

Diana responds:

> The truth is that for every person sitting in this circle, *we can't wait to see where it takes you either (5)!* As a matter of fact, we are jealous! We've seen the changes happen but we've only see it as a change. When I think about you, Alex, and my daughter, there is the reality that you've been born into, which means that *you are going to be so much freer from some of the fears and prejudices that hold us back (6).* Your ability to move into this map of the future is like, "Well, that's just my life!" That means that you're going to be able to be much more creative with all this than we can ever hope to be. For anybody here who has helped this path open for you, we are profoundly grateful for that. We just want you to have fun! *We want you to have a really good time making the future! We'll stand with you as long as we're around (7).*

1. Where do you touch down in this conversation about the passage of time? We've identified seven distinct points of view to facilitate your conversation (the numbers in parentheses following each underlined statement). Which of those speak to you?

2. What seems to be missing for you from this discussion of the emerging future and our relationship to it?

Diana tells us about her experience of visiting a United Church of Christ congregation in Seattle* a year ago. She thought they were gutsy in asking her to speak about *awakening* when most congregations and conferences are asking Diana to speak about decline or theological changes. Diana did her preparation for the presentation without knowing that the congregation was also getting ready for her visit by initiating an art show in which congregational members were invited to create something that would symbolize awakening. When Diana arrived, all the pieces were on display in the church. It was spectacular! Having visited many of the pieces, Diana talks about walking to the front of the church—the chancel—where there was a long table with sixteen chairs around it. At first she didn't get the way that this "winning" piece referenced the theme of awakening, but then the person accompanying her revealed the significance of the chairs to her.

> *And I looked, and there were 13 chairs for all the people who were missing from the table. There was a chair decorated for the children who have been born with terrible disfigurement. There was a chair for service people who had come back from Afghanistan and Iraq and how they felt lost. There was a chair for transgendered people who have no space in our conversation.*

> *See! That's the point of Awakening: pulling up more chairs to the table. Awakening is never about sending people away from the table. In all the world's great religious traditions, when we talk about awakening, it's always about bringing more and more people to God's table.*

> *From all my travels talking about this in the last two years, that was the greatest learning moment: Imagining what God's table is going to look like when it is really filled.*

> *When I go out now and people ask me to talk about the decline of the church, I'm only willing to do so insofar as it leads us to more chairs at the table.*

> *That's what Awakening is.*

What chairs would *you* place at the Table of Awakening?

*Kris Garratt, Liturgical Artist at University Congregational United Church of Christ, reports that the table and chairs were temporarily in place in the chancel in place of the regular communion table when Diana lectured there. In shaping this community arts project, she first asked the congregation to provide written input on who they wanted to see seated at the table and what nourishment should be available on the table itself. Based on their input, she collaged 13 chairs (the chairs themselves were repurposed/recycled from one of our church programs). She was very intentional about doing 13 chairs to make a connection to traditional stories of the last supper with Jesus and the disciples. She invited some church members who have regularly helped her with art projects over the years to help finish collaging the table. The installation has travelled to other locations to be used interactively in worship services, which is the way she loves to see it used.

OPTION 4: PERSONAL AWAKENING
(a process of closing reflection at the end of the series)

What will you take away from this 5-session experience of learning with Diana Butler Bass? The discipline of naming personal learning at the end of a series like this is an important one both for individuals who carry the change into their community and for the group that has been the birthplace of those awakenings. Here are some things that were named by the members of the group that met with Diana in Alexandria:

From Greg:

What was especially powerful for me was the change in the belonging question from "Who are you?" to "Whose are you?"

From Stephanie:

Even when my neighbors are part of that large "unaffiliated" group, I will still see them as children of God and as people through whom I can have a closer relationship with God.

From Alex:

As time goes on and things are changing and I find myself living the challenges that accompany change, I will treat these things as positive forces that can help me and shape me. As C.J. said, "Being Christian isn't easy!" but it's worth it.

From Sharon:

This has provided me with new words and ideas that will enable me to accompany friends and connect more deeply with those who identify as spiritual but not religious.

From C.J.:

I take away a new appreciation for people who are affiliated with religion in ways that I am not. The road map you have offered, Diana, offers guidelines for a journey where we all carry our own maps.

From Marilyn:

I am going to expand my sense of neighborhood so that I can grow beyond the limitations I had previously drawn that left others out of the circle as well as beyond the assumptions I had made that left me out.

1. What will *you* take from this series of five sessions featuring the teaching of Diana Butler Bass?

3. What do you want to do next?

2. What appreciations do you have for the members of the community that have accompanied you?

OPTION 5: LIVING CONVICTION THROUGH PRACTICE WITH NEIGHBORS
(an option for personal reflection following the session)

Following the session you will continue to think about issues raised both on the DVD and in your small group. This suggestion is offered to support you in continuing the integration of learning beyond the end of this series.

Use these stems as a way of continuing to reflect on the key elements of this session and this series:

- As I engage in living a dynamic faith, I am convicted that...

- I take these spiritual practices to deepen my own awakening...

- I choose to bring a chair to the table for these neighbors...

One: Presence of Possibilities,
All: Open us with holy surprise.

One: Source of Imagination,
All: Color us outside the lines.

One: Nearness of Neighbor,
All: Dance us into spacious love.

One: Abundance of Choice,
All: Convict us into mattered living.

One: Path of Pilgrimage,
All: Walk us into spirited experience.

One: Mystery of Emergence,
All: Startle us into awakening.

One: Practice of Presence,
All: Be our eternal Now. *Amen.*